The Grace of Neces

D0174487

Other titles by Samuel Green:

Gillnets (Cold Mountain Press)
Wind (Breakwater Press)
Hands Learning to Work (Brooding Heron Press)
Vertebrae (Grey Spider Press)
Keeping Faith (Grey Spider Press)
Communion (Grey Spider Press)
VERTEBRAE: Poems 1978-1994 (Eastern Washington University Press)
Working in the Dark (Grey Spider Press)
The Only Time We Have (Grey Spider Press)

THE

GRACE

OF

NECESSITY

∽

S<small>AMUEL</small> G<small>REEN</small>

Carnegie Mellon University Press, Pittsburgh, 2008

ACKNOWLEDGMENTS

Many of these poems first appeared in the following anthologies & periodicals:

Poetry Prairie Schooner; Longhouse; Great River Review; Tailwind; Fragments; Poetry East; Cistercian Studies Quarterly; Origin; Touch Me There: A Yellow Silk Book (Warner, 2000); Denise Levertov: New Perspectives (Locust Hill Press, 2000); Bestiary (Evergreen State College, 2002); This Should Be Enough (Skagit River Poetry Festival, 2002); The Sound Close In (Skagit River Poetry Festival, 2004)

"What the Fisherman Knows" was produced as a limited edition booklet commissioned by Wessel & Lieberman Booksellers, Seattle.

"Grubs" & "Psalm" were produced as broadsides by WoodWorks Press, Seattle. "At the Pond's Edge" was produced as a broadside by Aralia Press, West Chester.

Other poems appeared in two chapbooks:

Working in the Dark (Grey Spider Press, 1998)
The Only Time We Have (Grey Spider Press, 2002)

Thanks to the editors for permission to reprint.

The author is grateful to a number of people during the writing of these poems, especially to the following: Kathy Shoop, Tim Bruce & the Skagit River Poetry Festival project; Donald Hall; Wendell Berry; Doug Thorpe; Paul Hunter; Alicia Hokanson; Barry Sternlieb; Laurel Rust; Phyllis Ennes; Tim McNulty; Bill O'Daly; Tom Sexton; Hayden Carruth; David Lee; Bill Ransom; Ted Kooser; Joe-Anne McLaughlin; Sean McDowell; Tony Curtis; Theo Dorgan; Paula Meehan; Katie Donovan; Jim McAuley. Particular thanks are due to Edwin Weihe, who hired me & first showed me Paris & Ireland, & to my colleagues at Seattle University. To Jules Remedios Faye & Chris Stern at Grey Spider Press, all gratitude for their continuing faith. My island neighbors have contributed more than they could know. Above all, thanks to my wife, Sally: one lifetime is not enough for love or homage; she makes all grace visible, belief reasonable, poetry possible.

Publication of this book is supported by a grant from the Pennsylvania Council on the Arts.

Library of Congress Control Number: 2007921262
ISBN 978-0-88748-501-5
ISBN 978-0-88748-479-7 Pbk.

10 9 8 7 6 5 4 3 2 1

for Sally & Lonnie
for Jules
& in memory of
Ken Brewer   Ellen Meloy
& especially
C. Christopher Stern

CONTENTS

1. Working in the Dark

2. Daily Practice, 2001-2002

3. The Only Time We Have

The Grace of Necessity

1. WORKING IN THE DARK

Miserere: That We Might Keep Her Present Among Us

for Taryn Hoover

Now, when the apples she might have picked against winter
are falling, let us recall her, let us pick them & eat.

Let us recall her as the leaves start their turning,
as seed pods of maples spin & drift in the fickle wind.

As the long vowels of rain spill from the sky's dark sack,
let us bring her back—not as a burden,

no knapsack of grief that will bend us—
but a velvet presence come from the spun cocoon of pain.

Let us recall her because we can, it is easy, the memory
collective, each story shared like bread, elemental as salt.

Let the stories gather as tiny birds
add themselves one & one to the flock,

their small throats gathering the One
Great Song that is more than themselves alone.

Now, in the shortening days when light unbraids
too early, let us astonish each other

with love, as though, through us, we channel her desire.
Let us summon her here that she be present

among us, because the true burden is absence,
because joy, O my neighbors,

can be grafted to loss & bring fruit everbearing,

         so that

though there is grieving,
there is never true separation, never a leaving.

Cemetery Work Bee

We do not know if time stops
for the dead, but for us the dead stop
in time, like the drowned child

who would be ninety-four, but stays
a child perpetual in our memories.
We speak to the dead with our labor.

They are not strangers, but neighbors,
though many were dead before our time
in the world, or in this place.

In this coming together we work from affection,
linking ourselves to them by choice.
With chainsaws & axes, bow saws & brush hooks,

we slash back the woods toward the fence, cleansing
with fire. We do not think it strange to make room
for more, & if some of us have a secret

desire for others to be here
before we follow ourselves, it is human
enough. Moss over marble, over sea rock,

old graves & new, & the hurt still is new
at their seeing. We rest & eat among them,
sharing our food & water while sweat dries

& breath comes more slowly.
We include the dead in our joking.
We tell them news. The oldest among us

knows names & their stories the rest of us don't,
& we listen. He speaks out the names
of those whose stones have faded

with rain & wind. How little time
means to them now, this one gone
eighty years, & that is nothing

when weighed against how long he will stay
gone. We do not loan the dead our bodies,
but the living who will be dead. We notice

which of our neighbors walks without care
over the graves, we file that knowledge away,
each of us knowing our places.

Grave Digging

We could be working in gardens, we four
men with shovels, grubhoes, picks. We bend
our backs & are through the soil laid down
in an old man's life with the first half slice
of a shovel blade. We work with an ease
that surprises, the banter of neighbors who come
at odd moments together. We stop to gawk
at an odd plaiting of clouds, make crude jokes
about the shapes of uncovered rocks,
curse at scuffed knuckles, a nick of flesh
from a finger, marvel at the size of roots
from trees long vanished.

If there is a moment of joy, it isn't when
the rest of our neighbors pass through the gate
& become a single murmur of mourning, or when
we lower the old man into the hole
& someone sings *The International*,
or when small boys begin moving the grave
mound with toy trucks, but that time,
over my head, deeply alone in the ground,
having dug a chamber off to the side
for the one stone too large to remove, I was catching
my breath in that gravity of silence, looked up
at men I suddenly knew might some day
dig a hole for me, lay my body in it, cover me
over, turn, & carry me away.

Winter Solstice, 1997

for Denise Levertov

My wife takes every candle in the cabin,
puts them on top the piano, the desk,
in all the corners, the counter
in the kitchen, lights every lamp
we own & turns the wicks up high.

The Christmas tree shines with burning
wax, the stove is undamped,
its fireproof glass door
a fixed & brilliant eye.

On this, the day of longest dark,
she celebrates the turn, the growing
strength of light to come.

We step out on the porch & gaze
back through the window which blazes
in brilliant glory from dozens of flames.

We didn't know she was one day
gone, that poet whose life was spent
"doing to things / what light does to them."
Not to dazzle, as with lesser poets,
but to cast out shadows as demons,
to *illumine* in the old sense.

How do we subtract her from the world
& keep the sum of ourselves?
Light links us to light.
We move into the winter of mourning,
to days lengthening with grief
& only the bright rooms of her books

to sustain us, those sparks struck
from the vast dark flint
that catches in us as tinder
till we, too, glow & glow, as the sender.

White Fir in Snow

for Donald Hall

Near the woodshed a white fir,
bent under snow
nearly to the ground
stays bowed,
even after the thaw.
The woods are full
of trees like this—cedar, hemlock, yew.

Year after year it happens,
the awful
weight, more, almost
than can be borne,
& then a lifetime struggling
upright again, drawn
by whatever light still filters
through the heavy canopy
of all those gone before.

Laying Stone

for Charlie Kiel

It is my tenth day of laying stone,
& my hands are scraped & cracked because
I need to feel the mortar with my skin.
Beneath our house, then, the long wall grows
in spite of the news of your dying.

I stand in the yard & breathe
beneath a sky the color of bruised flesh,
& stare at the rocks at my feet.
Some nearly too large to lift. Some
the size of my fist. Others no bigger
than the knot you tied in
the rope that unburdened you finally.

Over & over we make our choices. Each
stone that is fit requires the faith another
will go beside, that the random pile
will provide, & there will be making
beyond what we could know.

Ten days of making stone love stone,
& my foolish fingers bleed, too sore to touch
anything harder than my wife's face without pain,
hefting the weight of your death, my friend,
letting it find its place, as the sky bears
down, contracts, & it rains.

The Work That Is Given

for Phyllis, in memory of Mary Luvera, 1905-2000

Here you are, at a tree prepared by her going
whose life was spent feeding others.
Husband & son & two daughters,
neighbors & strangers, family or friends: for them
her hands had work in them always,
having come from a time that believed
hands are the tools of the heart,
that you do the work you are given.

And yours will be used as she taught you,
pruning the lush tree of grief branch by branch
until love, like small birds, can pass through
from any direction. What grows there then
will be rich & full of light. You will take nothing
without thinking how it must be given away.

What the Fisherman Knows

for those who loved Steve Sherman (1954-1999)

He knows that,
for all their muscled
power, their range,
the salmon cannot know
when they will suddenly
be called back
by something beyond
their understanding,

he knows there's no guarantee
that hooks or nets,
no matter how lovingly made
or cunningly set, can hold them
when they give themselves up
to that calling,

he knows they can slip past,
& that there's nothing to do then
but let them go back to the source
recalling the way
the sea parted before them, their brief
but startling flash
in the sun when they leap
on their way toward a stillness
no storm could ever reach.

Bearing the Word

You could try holding a ripe quail's egg
in your teeth & jogging across broken
ground until you can do it without cracking
the shell; you could try wrapping your tongue
in tar-soaked gauze & chanting spells
you somehow know would heal
if only you could say them
cleanly; try gathering the shards
of Anisazi pots from the tops of a dozen mesas
& then begin the work of assembling
a single one from all those parts
until it will hold stone-
filtered water; do this blindfolded.
                              Nothing, nothing
can prepare you to carry the words
that tell your wife her sweet, beloved
mother is dying. There is nothing but the daily
practice of being full as a barrel
catching rain from a clean roof,
to which she can come as her own
terrible thirst requires.

Nearly Automatic Writing: Testimony of My Great Grandmother

The Indians I grew up with call me
'Sibitzibe,' *little mouse*. My neighbors,
in their gossip & tales, call me 'Shotgun Mina.'
Which, I wonder, am I?
My second husband, Guiseppi,
held his tongue when I showed him
my old 12-gauge, the bores
looking like two small mouse doors.
I am done with husbands, done
with names.

***

A screaming cougar, they say, sounds
like a crying child. It doesn't. It sounds like
a mad woman screeching out
a loneliness. I have heard myself
scream like that, sometimes, inside
my head.

***

Two of the children climbed the high island off LaPush,
the tribe's last refuge in attack, the narrow, rocky
trail impassable to an enemy. At the top
there's a spring. Hazel said her brother found a skull
there, & offered her a drink from the mossy cap
of bone. My own head ached all day, the way a drink
of cold ice melt from the river makes it ache.

***

Father was here for a visit, wearing
his Salvation Army uniform
with its Captain's insignia. He spoke fiercely
of God while I looked past him through the window.
Crows in the compost, caterwauling. It does no good
to chase them off. No matter which door
in the house I open, the sentry finds me out,
& they are all soon safe in the cedars.
They can kill even a large thing,
starting with the eyes
& then working away at their leisure.
How to send my father,
with his words like crows, black & sharp-beaked,
away? How to say the difference between
love & obedience? The crows stand & stay.

***

Walking downriver, I met a bull
elk blocking the way, the water too high
to wade, & high bank on my right, a fallen fir
angling steeply up. It wasn't his being there
that angered me, & I could have stood it
had he seemed the least aggressive,
but he barely acknowledged my presence,
went on browsing the sweet willow
when I stamped my foot & hollered at him
to move. I went up that fallen tree
as nimble as you please when he charged,
then sat on the bank while he bucked,
snorted, shook his head, & scraped against bark
the jagged antler, the brow tine
I'd broken off with the biggest stone
I could manage to throw.

***

The children brought a seal pup home, pulled
from the rocks between high waves. I scolded them,
but let them place it in a box by the cook stove,
the way we do sometimes with a young pig.
We fed it milk fresh
from the evening's chores. It
drank, though not with any greed
I could see. When the children slept,
I took a lamp to the kitchen. The fire
was down to coals, stove top ticking
like a skipping heart as the metal
cooled. I think I expected to find it
dead, but when I brought the lamp near
enough to push away the shadows
it was watching me through one great eye.
It reminded me of my sister
on her deathbed. Whenever we entered
the room we stepped into her eyes.

It was two more days before the body caught up
with what the mind already knew
& the hurt thing died. When I skinned it
I found a great bruise on its left side, the ribs broken.
Oh, & I carry wounds as fierce,
though skinning wouldn't show them.

***

We went to the beach for mussels. The big
blue ones. I found a pearl in one of mine,
misshapen. It has, though, a cruel
beauty. You can imagine something like this
made from pain. In its way, it is more honest
than those the fancy ladies wear.
It could be a symbol for my own life.

On Board the *Sea Lassie*, Summer, 1944

I can bring back the boat, a purse seiner
built in the 20s, white, paint flaking
from her rails. She has made her set
& swings like a clapper against
the enormous bell of Alaskan sky.

I can bring back the gulls floating
like flakes of dirty snow sternward,
the smell of leaked diesel, the sound
of the hull scraped with the weight
of tarred cotton & fish.

I can bring back the crew, & I do,
a small group of mostly older men with the ghosts
of their lives in their mouths, the tall Swede
still sweating out last night's whiskey. They smell
of tobacco smoked or chewed, the sour stench
of unbathed bodies, coffee, & too much grease
in their food.

My father is easy: there are pictures of him then
at seventeen, handsome, high boots & a rubber
apron, black-billed hat tipped back, bare arms
as yet without tattoos. Because he is who he is
he is watching the coastline for bears
on the beach. Because he is already
who he will become, he is also doing his job
braced against spray & pitch,
though not neatly enough for his father.

Having brought them here, there is still
nothing I can do about my grandfather's hands,
those knuckles hard as barnacles slamming
into my father's face, knocking him down
& onto the hatch cover, again

& again, because he keeps getting up,
too young & strong & full of pride
to simply stay hunched on the deck.

I bring my father back because I want
to tell that boy he will not beat
his own two sons, & they will not
beat theirs, to tell him though he'll mourn
the fact he cannot mourn his father's death,
I know I'll weep for his. But the boy can't hear me.
He has become an old man in whom pain
has lived like a flapping salmon in his ruined back
his whole life long. I could tell *him*, & try
whenever I visit. But that's not the same thing, is it?

Wood Splitting

Why spend so much
careful time with the file
on the axe, shaping
the steel to that exact
bevel, & then the rough
stone with oil, honing
& honing & honing,
switching to the fine stone,
the silkier feel,
then finally the leather
to take away the burr,
when nearly always
I use the heavy maul,
blunt, clumsy, dull, & depending
on a sort of cold fury?

Teaching My Son to Kill

Doe in a fall orchard steps among trees in heavy
rain. We are waiting for the buck to leave the brush &
meet her there to mouth apples
fallen into the high grass.
So. She is here, & we are, & the
long shadows grow longer. No matter. We are here to
teach my son to wait, & about light fading. What the
doe, & the buck, know well enough.

At Least the Rabbits

Here, at the garden's edge, where kale
has diminished morning
after morning, where tufts of fur
& only a little blood describe
the grass, something stopped being
what it was, & began the journey
toward becoming other.

If you think your heart is a sleeping hen
you spend your nights in fear of owls, clustered
tight with the rest of the flock.

At least the rabbits move into the open,
at least they go about their business,
at least they take their chances with the hawks.

Grubs

Working with the bark spud
peeling cedar logs for the shed
I uncover white grubs,
wrinkled & thick as my little finger.
They have powerful jaws.
Working in the dark, blind, in faith
toward whatever they might become,
they leave delicate etchings
in the wood. I have to say
that I understand them
more than the squawking, squabbling
chickens who crowd in to peck them
from my unprotected hand.

Skates, West Beach Resort

It was a small girl saw them first,
    & those of us out for a late walk
down the dock leaned against the rail

to see what we could in the pools of light
    the flood-lamps made. The bottom
was littered with offal,

dead crabs belly up, fish heads,
    the spines of fish with only tail
& flaps of skin attached. And among them

the skates, a dozen dark shapes gliding
    above the mud, wide wings rippling
like silk shrouds, liquid in liquid,

thin tails undulating,
    a trail of murk behind them, shadows
into insubstantial light into shadow,

as we are plunged suddenly into ourselves,
    none of us looking at another, each watching
in silence, as tiny waves lick away the beach.

Children, Waking

for Laura Walker

In the long night, when our sons wake
& their cries come
through our thin sleep so we rise then
from our love's side
& we move off through the held breath
of the still house
where we lift them from their wet beds
just to hold them
through the strained dark with their warm weight
in our curled arms,
if we walk then, or we rock them,
through our mouths come
all the soft songs from our own past,
whether sleep songs
or the sweet hums that propel them
toward our best hopes,
though the truth is that we can't take
either sickness
or their grief-hurts into our selves,
though we wish to
& we try to, all we can do
is to soothe them
through the worst time, for it's our flesh
held in our flesh
& it won't stop when they leave us
though they can't know
that we still sing through the house walls
when the stars call
till our fears still & the heart sleeps
in the long will that the night keeps.

What's Brought Back

for Ken Brewer

Two nights ago a neighbor stepped from sleep,
into his meadow to pee & heard
what he thought were whales singing
to the moon from North Bay.

For half an hour he listened,
goose bumps on his thighs,
nipples tight with the night
chill, shutting out the chorus
of frogs in the swamp, persistent
owls, skitter of rats in the woodpile,
the muskrat chewing at tubers
in the pond. When the sound
stopped, there was nothing
to measure it by
except its absence.

All evening I've been lying in bed surrounded
by sounds I can't put aside: a lone mosquito
that's whined through an unseen gap in the screen
door; the small engine of a plane dying
away to the east; gusts of wind shaking furies
of rain from the cedar onto the roof
above my head; the cracks of drying wood
in the log walls of this house I made.

I've been reading your poems for hours, a gesture
of love to keep away this day when light begins
to fail, a day when you are ill, where little
can be done, where every poem you've made is a gift
that takes us away from you, song by song,
brings us back to ourselves & the noisy singing
world you've loved so well, so long.

For Hayden, Ill
Summer, 2000

Do they have prickly sow-thistle out where
you live, Hayden? Or in Vermont, where your
heart in large part still abides? We say
heart when we mean *spirit* or *soul* or *love*,

but it's your actual heart that's suddenly
off exploring new rhythms the way you have
your whole life. And for those of us across
the country who love you, we pay the cost

of distance & wait. I pass my time with work,
grunting the wheelbarrow from woods to house
& back, thirteen eight foot ricks to get us
through our mild northwest winter. This is work

you know. Only the trees are different: big
leaf maple, red alder, white & Douglas fir,
all split & seasoned & ready to brag
about in stacks I fit to shed rain or

snow past the tarps, stand against gravity
or wind. Good practice for poets. To me
you've often lamented the loss in your life
of physical labor, you, whose neighbors might

have hired Hayden-the-Handyman, part-time
tinkerer & mechanic. And you still
are, too. All these years how many poems
have you tinkered with for others? Well,

but I know what you mean, & wondered, too,
how work has found its rhythms in your poems:
the lift & swing of axe or maul, the slow
push & pull of a Swedish saw, the two-time

slap & pause of nailing shingles on a roof.
Mornings, before another dawn comes wriggling
improbably from the magician's stiff
black hat, I read your words by the lighting

of a kerosene lamp. The lines stay clear
in my head as the wheelbarrow wears a path
through the clearing we seeded with grass
once the trees had been felled for the house. Hear

that slick hiss, Hayden? Awhile ago I
had to stop, take the wheel apart, & pack
the bearings with grease. Yesterday I patched
my leather gloves with waxed thread. We never try

to sort the work from leisure: a cheek
full of mint, warm raspberries in the hand,
a swig of well water from the canteen
hanging on a branch in the shade. And

when I tilt my head to drink, there's a hawk
that floats like an eyelash across the flawless
blue iris of sky. I have found my place
in the world, as you did once, by good luck,

or grace, or example. Like prickly sow-
thistle, with its tall green stalk that bleeds
milk when it's cut. The field guides call them weeds,
of course, but I love their honest yellow

flowers, a lot like dandelions, or
hairy cat's ear. Like your poems, your heart, they're
stubbornly in the world, having learned
the art of the marginal: do everything

well. In their time, the bright tops turn
to seed balls, a cluster of light shimmering
parachutes that fluff, loosen, & trust
42   the wind. We find what loves us, & persist.

2. DAILY PRACTICE
2001—2002

Aug. 26

A dragonfly lights on the tip
of a dead elderberry branch.
From time to time it leaps
to grab a gnat, then settles
again. It seems a minor thing
until the sun clicks forward
one more notch
& pours itself through
a single tilted wing.

Aug. 30

This far toward fall, the wildlife
gets more intense. A pileated
woodpecker cackles like a mad
uncle for minutes. Crows
resent the least intrusion. Hornets
& wasps hum heavily as they hunt
the clearing for grubs. Across the island
one chainsaw grumbles to life. Another
answers. Another.

Sept. 8

Evening, just before sunset,
the highest trees to the south
are dipped in bronze. Light thickens
them. Like honey. Amber. It sweetens
the dusk, mocks the gathering shadows.

Sept. 9

A nuthatch slams into the bay
window. The ledge catches her,
keeps her from the cat's mouth,
but she stays there, stunned, caught
by the betrayal of air turned suddenly
solid. How could she ever move
past this moment without the grace
of necessity? How could any of us?

Sept. 11

The rain-split plums
have been falling, the ground
so littered now that numbers
no longer have meaning.

Sept. 12

We keep the radio off, sit
by the window & listen to bamboo
chimes, the ping of string
beans sealing in their cans,
trying to still the voices inside us.

Sept. 14

Light alone can't unlock the mourning.
Everything we see carries
the burden of what we know
until we let it be itself again. Walking
the yard with coffee cooling
in my hand, I stop at a single seed
of hawkbeard balanced
on a blade of grass. Except
for paying attention, what else
is continual prayer?

Sept. 16

Out in the Channel the tankers are sounding
their horns, finding their way. The weather
seems appropriate. All day
we murmur to one another, trying
to find our way through
grief. "We must love one another,"
said Auden, "or die." Years later
he threw this away as a lie, saying
that all of us die anyway, having lost
the sense to see how many deaths there are
worse than the one he imagined.

Sept. 18

Walking into the dark
away from the radio, feet
muffled on the dirt roads. Wind bears
the names of what is dear: here is
owl, it says—barred owl, great horned,
the tiny screech—here is rabbit-through-the-brush.
Others. It doesn't bear the names
of the lost, any more than we can.

Sept. 19

We walk through trees in darkness,
trusting what we know
& our linked hands
to guide us home. On the trail,
yellow leaves float toward us
like *koi* from a deep black pond, rising
the way love rises.

Sept. 23

Chickadee in the birdbath
dips, shakes, twitches left,
right, left, darts away, back,
furtive. Any shadow or shape
could become cat, hawk.
Only by choice do we say no
to that.

Sept. 27

Dumping the kitchen scraps
in the compost, surprise
a rat, which wants to become
part of the gray board wall
he's trapped against. He looks
so tired, old, & so beautifully
part of the grain that I leave him
there to cobs & peelings & grounds,
a world of owls, cats, of cold, cold rain.

Sept. 28

Sometimes the rain
on the roof is such a balm
to pain, the sound of it drowning
out all the other sounds
until we simply give in
to it. Today, it is not enough.
Too much drought
in too many hearts.
Listen: the ground takes everything
that comes. Everything.

Oct. 1

It's hard, sometimes, standing
in the orchard, peeling an apple
with my grandfather's knife
watching the sweet spirals of
color fall away from the blade
& no small boy standing there
with a story between him
& all that sweet white meat.

Oct. 2

Just after first light one
of the cats lets himself
through the pet door, mouth
full of sparrow, & we notice
nothing until it screams.
The cat eludes us, back
outside in a flash of fur.
The sound stays in the house
all day, fluttering from wall to wall.

Oct. 8

The radio says that bombs
are falling again in our name.
At lunch, I suddenly can't bear
to make the knife dice
the vegetables. Steamed whole,
they stay in the pot, grow cool, grow
cold, grow colder.

Oct. 9

More important this morning
than coffee, is the cup
I drink it from, made
by someone who loved
good clay, a simple glaze
enough.

Oct. 12 Anacortes

Downtown, main street,
a hawk hangs on a wire,
leaning against the wind,
feathers fanning. Sometimes
there is nothing to do
but hold on.

Oct. 13 Seattle

The television is merciless
in its images, the repeating
of them, war become a battle
of ratings, each nuance of each act,
each syllable of speech
examined & pecked at, like
the body of the dead cat
in the restaurant parking lot, the gathered
& gathering crows.

Oct. 16 Olympia

The car radio says we are still
killing. The words come so easily
from her lips. Practice, practice.
A dead gull lies in the lane
in front of us, one wing rising
& falling in the small wind.

Oct. 17 New York City

At Battery Park my friend
& I lean into a harsh wind
while he points out the Statue
of Liberty. Behind us, armed soldiers
in forest camouflage are grimly watching.
We are fresh from Ground Zero, & coughing
into the wind. Neither of us mentions
what it is comes out of our lungs.

Oct. 18 New York City

On the subway an old
Polish man takes me in charge,
rides two stops past his own
to make certain I find
the right place to get off. When I try
to thank him, he shakes his head
no, forget it. No one, he says,
should be lost when someone else
knows the way.

Oct. 26

When I step into the yard
to dump the chamber pot,
it is quiet. Even my neighbors'
roosters haven't renewed their sovereignty
yet. I imagine all the trees in the orchard,
the ones we dug holes for, set a rich
meal of dark soil & compost & rotted
manure for, watered in the dry times—these,
I say, I imagine bowing slightly
to acknowledge me as I pass,
having stood through another night
of wind. Who would not laugh at himself
at such thoughts, pouring his own piss
into eggshells, potato peels, the odd
scraps we hope to turn into something
we wish so badly could love us?

Oct. 30

What I hear:
rain falling on the roof, running
from the gutters; rain on the woodpile
tarps; the clock's tick; wood
popping & hissing in the stove; the breath
of all three cats; each page Sally turns
in her book upstairs; occasional creak
of the house; the scratch of my pen
across this paper; the low hiss
of kerosene in the lamp; half a dozen
silent chainsaws on my neighbors' porches.

Nov. 2

From the bedroom window
we can see the full moon
to the west criss-crossed
with branches. It lights
the room, but cannot see
what we do in that light.

Nov. 7

In a corner by the press, a spider hikes
the slope of a seal's skull we found
on the beach. The silence of any bone
is profound, but more so this box
that held the brain & eyes. On the desk
an eagle's skull, a hawk's on the piano,
a small owl's, we think, on a shelf
above the window. Nothing in the house
is so still.

Nov. 17

Another yellowjacket queen wakes
in the heat of the house & makes
for the nearest window, barely able to stay
in the air, a drunken hope. Nothing
can save her, so we are gentle,
catching her in tissue
as light as her wings, & letting her go
outside into the indifferent cold.

Dec. 5

Wind shakes the trees like a cat
with a dead bird. Playful. No harm
meant at all, leaves scattering
like feathers.

Dec. 6

Boiling potatoes for lunch. The window
above the stove mists over. I practice
calligraphy on the glass with the tip
of my finger, like a boy
in love, see the yard outside
through our initials, the flourishing
ampersand, the heart surrounding.

Dec. 17

Out to dump the slops, stop
by the bamboo to hear
what it sounds like in the rising
wind, startled by a tree frog calling
from under a thin curl of bark.
I am not the answer it wants.

Dec. 19

Dry air. A *snap* at the tip
of my finger when I touch
the damper of the stove, a *snap*
when I go to turn
the English muffin, *snap*
adjusting the wick
of the lamp, & a *snap*,
jolt, & a blue spark
caught in the mirror of the window
with our morning kiss.

Feb. 15 La Conner

There: one man walking
across a field, geese rising
before him as he goes. They never
stand their ground. He never slows.

March 21 Anacortes

No sign of the heron this morning, but
a thin skin of ice on the swamp pens
a pair of mallards to one end
which they have probably kept open
all night with their bodies. Now
the hen is moving in small
circles, the drake nearly lost
against the green of the swamp
grass, as I am nearly lost,
but for the space she keeps open inside me.

March 26 Mount Vernon

A possum by the roadside, head
in the ditch, so wet its fur
doesn't move at all in the wind
a passing truck makes.

March 31 Easter
Padilla Bay Dike

Even without the bright slashes
of crimson among the thorns
we would recognize him
by his voice, the rising
joy of a single red
winged blackbird.

April 9

The one early plum
in the orchard has bloomed,
the flower girl gone to school
in the dress that she wore
to the wedding.

April 10

The sickle is so sharp
that it sings as it cuts:
thwing through nettles, *thwing*
through thimbleberry, salmonberry,
elderberry, *thwing thwing*
the fresh shoots of maple & wild
cherry, the steel bright
in the sun, the handle freshly oiled
against the long work waiting.

April 11

One neighbor is nailing boards, three raps
to a nail. Steady hand. Another is using
a planer—long planks, by the length
of the whine. Three chainsaws are growling
through next winter's wood, all these sounds
echoing off the outhouse walls.

April 12

A small frog hitches a ride
on my neck from the woodpile
to the front deck, gets off
at the lilac, disappears
into silence.

April 13

Tea steams in the lamplight.
Scent of oranges the color
of coals glowing in the glass
door of the stove. The radio
is off. Across pages the color
of clouds, words of Chinese poets
fly like geese coming home
from a long winter.

April 14

Dawn, & all those feathered bodies
eager to name themselves: thrush,
robin, sparrow, a rush of notes
tumbling like creek water
over stones, or short notes
like the sharp & breathless delight
of lovers. Even the smallest wren strains
as though it believes its voice
is the one that sings the world into being,
as though it's a long time to dusk,
& the lamentation of silence.

April 19

All I know is that the bell
hung by the bird feeder rang
twice, & there is no wind
to move the clapper, no
visitor come knocking after
at the door. And when I blundered
down the stairs to look, there was nothing
unusual to see. All day I carried the sound
of that bell in my head, its brassy
assurance, wondering how badly I needed
to hear it, & how much it needed
to be heard.

April 20

Pruned the dead canes back
from last year's berries; mowed
the yard & orchard; cleaned
the mower; cut back brush
for an hour; sharpened
the sickle twice; & tracked
the spotted slug lugging its self-
contained intentions slowly,
slowly across the clearing.

April 21

On the windowsill, struggling
on its back, a beetle fallen
from a hole in the wall. Iridescent green,
copper. It shimmers in the soft
light. Listen: its cousins are tunneling
through the logs of the house with a terrible
hunger, taking their bright beauty
with them in the hard dark.

April 24

How odd the scream of an eagle
slicing through the clearing
should sound so much like
the cry of a hurt rabbit,
like brakes worn down
to metal, a nail pried
from a roof of galvanized tin,
something that doesn't want
to let go, letting go
again & again.

April 27

My love has scrubbed the windows-O,
& I have swept the floor.
My love has dumped the ashes-O,
while I chopped wood for more.
My love has done the dishes-O,
& I have fixed her tea.
My love has dumped the chamber pot
& cleaned it prettily.
My love has pulled the covers back,
& softened up the pillow.
We'll both lie down together there
& rise up whole tomorrow.

Cinco de Mayo

In this single six-inch square
of ground: a curl of bark from wild
cherry, antennae of an earwig
trembling at its edge; scattered needles
of Doug fir; a carrion beetle the color
of dried blood; tuft of plantain; downy breast
feather from some small bird. Each day I practice
the vocation of saying *yes*
& fail—or how could I ever make it
across the yard?

May 7

Chocolate lily, sea blush, calpyso
orchid, blue camas: as though
naming them could call up the colors,
the way they collect light
& spray it back across
the meadow, open-mouthed.

May 8

Someone else is up early, chainsaw
winning the argument with geese
at Adams' pond. Someone thinking
about winter & putting thought
into action, pausing now & again
maybe, at the sound of my maul
ringing against the wedge.

May 13

Like the petals of Scotch Broom
opening, hood within hood, between the thumb
& finger, the stamens snapping
out; like the stalks of wild coral root;
like the soft slap of wingbeats
on the waters of the bay, like
the two porpoise we watched off the point
rising in unison, their wet breath
one breath—a *whuff*—as they arced
into the light: a thousand other things
our bodies translated in the night.

June 3

Grass to my waist in the orchard,
hands blistered with the mowing.
A small frog leaps for safety
in front of me, leaps
& is lost, leaps & is lost.

June 5

Blow out the lamp & the moths quit
fluttering against the glass
before the wick stops glowing. That other
sound? Words flapping at the dim pane
of the mind long into darkness.

June 6

Sharpening the sickle again, bastard file
first, lightly, beveled on one edge, flat
on the back. Then the coarse stone with spit,
harsh sound, the metal scratching, a bright shore
along the rusted bay of blade. Then oil
& the fine stone, sound of skates on ice
perhaps, *shush, shush* the ragged burr
drawn out & away. Finish with linseed oil
rubbed in the oak handle, & then
to the dulling of brush, weeds, & grass.

June 9

Sally comes in salty from sun
& work in the garden where a blue
iris is blooming, a hummingbird
hanging in front of the parted
lips, the impossible pace of his tongue
a contrast to the storm
of his wings, his furiously greedy heart.

June 12

That sound in the late afternoon
that hangs above the clearing
without locus has to be
more than the weary drone
of bees in the berries, more
a moan than a hum,
the unexpected groan of lovers
approaching what doesn't want
to let them go.

June 17

Blossoms of foxglove hang
like church bells, bumblebees
swaying inside like clappers
that do not quite touch the sides.

June 19

One secret is to want
what the world is. The lilac
blooms turn brown? We love
their airy lightness, their pastel
freckles scattered on the raised grain
of cedar boards on the deck. A hemlock
breaks off in the wind? The light is better,
say. By such small deceits
the beauty of grief is put away.

June 29

Red ants move through the skull
of the dead rat by the fig tree
like monks cleaning
the floor of a sacred cave, carting away
the clutter, putting to use
what is useful, leaving finally
only an empty vault, open-mouthed,
shaping the summer air.

July 11

In my half sleep the owls
are Japanese poets chanting
their poems to one another,
five syllables, four, a dependable
form to celebrate silence,
hunger, & always
that concise competence.

July 22

A honeyed moon dribbles
light through cedars. Notes
from a neighbor's recorder sift
through brush. Night birds huddle
in a deep pocket of silence. Every leaf
along the road is still. Gravel mumbles
under my shoes. Inside my head
words tumble & crunch telling me
where, & who I am.

3. THE ONLY TIME WE HAVE

At the Pond's Edge

I come to her the way I'd come
to a pond's edge in October dusk
so as not to frighten the wood ducks.

My hands move on her flank like a drake
drifting across a pond's surface
or the slow caress of mist at dawn

hanging now on, now above the still water.
Dusk or dawn, a man *can* be gentle,
always & all ways gentle,

& still be a man, her slow teaching
over long years, the classroom her body,
nearly a quarter of a century now,

no longer the body's daily insistence,
the hard urgings that caused me once to
fear my own desire. We have slid

into middle age with sweet understanding,
the pleasure of the long familiar,
a tenderness that still

explodes into sudden wings on the water,
catching us both by surprise.

Winter Bath

"I am my beloved's, & my beloved is mine."
                    —Song of Songs

By lantern light I see her sway
through steam rising from
the water. Her robe comes away
in my hands, her body smelling
like the life we lead here:
typewash, ink,
the onions she sliced for the soup,
the understated promise
of garlic. Her breasts lift
in the water. Why do I want to say
they are like two moons,
when all I ever want them to be
is what they are? We obey the laws
of bodies, my orbiting hands, grateful
for the gravity that reaches, pulls,
& hauls us down.

When the True Beloved Goes

When a guest leaves,
no matter how loved,
the house seems lighter
as though one had
more room in one's skin.
But when
the True Beloved goes,
what weight descends,
what stillness,
& only the promise
of return
to keep the walls
from falling in.

Some Things You Missed
While You Were Away

Two hours of picking up windfall
apples in the bed
you planted with flowers
& herbs; how when I woke
in the night, there was the scent
of apples & mint
on my hands
instead of you.

***

When I pulled the blue
tarp from the apple press:
the smell.

***

One night short of its fullness,
giant rings of color around the moon,
me standing naked in the yard
after dumping the chamber pot
stunned
long enough to start shivering
& only the fire
in the stove
to bring me back.

***

A night so quiet
just after I blew out the lamps
I tracked the long scrape & rattle
of a single leaf
falling from the highest branches

of a maple near the laundry shed
my hands still as I listened.

***

Out for a walk just before daybreak
I saw an owl
grab a rabbit from the side of the road.
All the way I thought not of its cry
like a slapped child,
but of its sudden
ceasing.

***

A handful of late raspberries
& strawberries from the garden,
& nothing but my hand
to take them
from my cupped hand.

***

After ten days of October sun
the sound of those first familiar drops
of rain on the roof
only hours before the dawn
of my last day without you.

***

While you were gone, you missed
these things. I would have
missed them, too,
without these lines to bring them back
& pass them on to you.

Barred Owl's Call

before dawn
jars us both
from thin sleep.
Note after note
without answer
without break.
The call it makes
is what wakes us,
but it's not
what keeps us
awake.

February Song

In the midst of the work day I see her,
gone out to gather eggs, begin to wander
the yard. Between her fingers

she rolls the buds
on the plum trees, bends
to touch the ground, eyes
the brilliant sun finally risen
above the trees
which have blocked it
since November.

She walks the yard with questions:

Where is the sun now?
Where will the light be?
What could a frost kill?
What needs me?

She sees beyond
the fig's bare branches,
the lichened gooseberry,
the empty cold frame.

What is living, what has died?
What can I get from this patch of dirt?
How much room for strawberry plants,
& where should I put the squash?

All winter she has kept the garden
in her head, this woman whose son
has grown & left her,

who has had no daughters
but soil & light & water.

Neither old nor young
she squats to touch a rising crocus,
egg cartons on the ground beside her.

P s a l m

Each morning I wake to a hunger
not food at my table or meaningful work
nor love for my neighbor can staunch.
Each morning a thirst that cannot be quenched
by light, by the deepest draught of water.

That I come to Him at all is through her,
who is the table who sets herself
over & over, who is a basket of fishes,
bread in the mouth,
a cool pitcher of wine
tipped
& pouring.

Apologia

"You're entirely too lustful all this talk about your wife.
I think you should go to mass & ask forgiveness."—Colleague
  for Edwin & Noreen

Forgive me, Lord, that in your house
I should think of my wife, how her body is bread
made flesh, that bread comes
from the living lemmas
of wheat, Lord, whose beards, whose coarse
hairs stir in the day's least exhalation,
how the stalk, taut with the rising
sap, sways, as though drunk,
beneath the touch of small birds,
the fluttery brush of wings, the grip
of feet, the tiny plucking bites,
& of dough, Lord, the nearly private
white of it, how it swells with the passion
of yeast, the smell of that on one's hands
held to the nose for pleasure;

Lord, forgive me that wine on the tongue
brings a vision of grapes that hang
heavy on vines planted on the naked
flanks of hills, swollen, musky,
of skins that burst, of juice that spills
onto ready ground, insects hanging
by their mouth parts at the sweet wet splitting,
the glad greeting of tongue
& nectar, the busy singing become
a single, dizzy hum under the sweet
& ministering sun;

forgive me, Lord, forgive
that the bread & wine
of this woman should bring me again
& again to know the greater body,
that the body is not a burden,
that the self can be lost
& found in the feast,
that I take my portion, my sacramental serving,
dazed with gratitude at this unearned grace,
knowing I can say no braided garland
of soft syllables, no purled necklace
of liquid sounds, no rosary
of words that are fervent, insistent,
or rapturous enough
in praise.

Some Reasons Why
I Became a Poet

Because I wanted to undo each stitch
in time, unravel the nine seams
that inhibit remembering; because I wanted
to roll a stone with such tenderness
that moss would grow & hold light
on all sides at once; because I wanted to teach
every old dog I saw a new set of tricks;
because I wanted to lead a blind horse
to water & make her believe her thirst
mattered; because I wanted to count
the chickens of grief & gain before they hatched;
because I never wanted to let sleeping cats lie
in wait beneath the birdbath; because
I wanted to close the barn door after the last
horse went grazing & know that something
important was left stalled inside; because
I wanted to welcome all Greeks & the desperate
bearing of their gifts; & because I couldn't stop
keeping my poor mouth open in a sort
of continual awe, trusting that flies, like
words, would come & go in their own good time.

Ars Poetica I

for Sam Todd, 1903-1990

Nothing I might do could keep the seals
from sliding off their rocks,
their wave-worn ledges
& into the water. To spot them there
is half gift, half the simple trick
of being ready to see.

I cannot row silently enough
to surprise them, & now we are in
the shallow channel between two
small islands, boulders
close under our hull. My son
in the stern is scared
we might hit something, caught
as we are in the suck
of ebb tide. The rocks

are a bird refuge, & the gull stench
spreads over us
like a heavy wing
in the day's heat. A few seals
bob among the bull kelp, wide-eyed
& wary, even as I struggle
to keep the bow straight
in the current. I've seen their look
before, when my grandfather
drove my brother & me over truck
roads in the Olympics above Grisdale,
a company town where he worked
as a cat skinner. His language sketched
the landscape beyond the windshield:

shot a buck along this road once
still got some in the freezer

see thet cedar stump? thew a track
offa the D-8 right there Lord God
foreman thew a fit I hadta laugh

hey ain't thet a funny snag? a fahr
few years back did thet you hafta watch it

And right then, deer—three does a hundred yards
past the snag—alert, gazing at us. Twice
it was elk browsing huckleberry. A black bear
clawing grubs from a log. And once only
a bobcat crouched on a limb above the river,
its eyes fixed & fiery. Always the litany
of landmarks before the animal, always
my grandfather's silent grin at our joy,
his own eyes on the road ahead, strong hands
at the wheel. My son leans over the gunwale
imagining rocks tearing the hull & doesn't see
the minke whale surface, blow, & roll
under, leaving a vapor that rainbows
briefly in the sun. With my grandfather's voice
I say, *What kind of boat is that*
toward Sandy Point? as we enter a tidal lee,
& my boy turns to look, surrounded
by the shy seals
he thought we came to see.

Ars Poetica II: Blade on Bone

He had read the line in a poem:
"the sound of a keen blade scraping bone,"
& felt the familiar shudder of exact
description. But, because he was feeling
pragmatic, he put down the book & walked
outside to the woodshed. He took
a goat's dried jawbone someone
had given him, & a seasoned stick
of hard maple from the cookstove
stack. His pocketknife had a fine
edge, he'd honed it on a round stone
& finished it with the leather strop. Tiny
white curls skirled from the blade's edge
as he scraped the bone, the same curls
came from the hard wood. He closed
his eyes, but the sound seemed
much the same. He held the jawbone
in his left hand, & saw how the teeth
were worn, thinking "the sound
of years chewed away," then hung it back
on its nail hook. Inside there was
the book, his place marked.
He returned to it, as
to something useful.

Ars Poetica III: A Neighbor Talks about Building Houses

Well, he says, I can do that, take the plans
another man's made in his head & make
a house. I built a place once like
that, exactly the way some goddamn

out-of-state architect specified,
a man who never laid good eyes on the land
& didn't know a thing about the kind
of rain we get up here, so the outside

rots, & the whole place just looks sort of stuck
there, gone limp, like one side of a man's face
after a stroke. Nope, what I like to do
is gather up stuff for a couple of

years: milled-up weirds & odds, some logs I love
for just their wild shapes, mixed woods, glass, a few
large stones. Then wait for place & need to take
hold, shake me up till I sit & think: Now,
what sort of house could all this make?

If You Had to

If you had to make the quill
pen in the old way, stripping
the feathers, cutting the well,
splitting & shearing the tip

off clean; if you had to grind
the ink, holding the cake
straight against the stone,
circling until your wrist ached

to get the proper tone of black;
would you wonder, as you sat before the paper
what sort of poem was worthy of your labor?

Scripsit

What, I wonder, made the slug
who left a lovely iridescent trail
up the trunk of the lilac, across
the cedar deck, diagonally across
the door, suddenly circle
on the window to leave

this perfect cursive "σ"
exactly the way that Mrs. Owens
taught me
forty-five years ago?

Abraham

It was not God
needed to know
what Abraham would do
with the knife in his hand,
his son bound on
the waiting wood,
but the man himself.

The ram he burned was
himself set free from
the awful thicket of doubt
the choking smoke of it
cleared away at last,
& for good.

Night Dive

Down here, no light but what we carry with us.
Everywhere we point our hands we scrawl
color: bulging eyes, spines, teeth or clinging tentacles.
At negative buoyancy, when heavy hands
seem to grasp & pull us down, we let them,

we don't inflate our vests, but let the scrubbed cheeks
of rocks slide past in amniotic calm.
At sixty feet we douse our lights, cemented
by the weight of the dark, of water, the grip
of the sea's absolute silence. Our groping

hands brush the open mouths of anemones,
which shower us in particles of phosphor
radiant as halos. As in meditation,
or in deepest prayer,
there is no knowing what we will see.

Getting By: Winter, 1984-85

So strum away on the old banjo,
keep that guitar hummin',
put more water in the soup,
there's better times a-comin'.
    —Folk Song

I.

In the thirties, following the hope
of work across country,
my mother's father stopped
at a store & stepped inside, bearing
his family's hunger
& their last quarter. He asked
for potatoes. The clerk
lugged a hundred pound sack
to the counter, went back
to the storeroom. My grandfather waited
for his measure. A while later
the startled clerk found him, patient
in the patched overalls of his poverty.

You still here?

All those bellies filled
while they lived in camps, worked
the fruit picking circuit, holding on
till the logging picked up at last.

2.

This is our third winter
on the homestead
& the hardest of weather, but a year
gone well: some work for cash,
bartered labor for shares

97

in several harvests. We canned
chickens, beans, tomatoes, put up
three kinds of fruit, made
pickled beets & sweet
zucchini relish. On the stove a goat
stew simmers through its second day.

Hundreds of icicles weigh the walls
of the tent house we live in. The canvas
sags, but the heat of two stoves has kept
the roof clear, & the storm has lagged—
that is, the heaviest snow has quit,
though the rough tongue of wind
still scuffs against us. I walk
out into the garden past the log walls
of the house we are building together,
scrape a place clear & slide the tines
of the fork into ground, lift
& turn. There are the round, small nubbins,
the fat, firm miracles.

Three more rows lie mulched
against frost, against ten inches
of snow. Inside we scrub the skins, slice
& add to the soup, mother & father
& small son, singing through the labor,
getting by through the only time
we have for certain, the only time we truly know.

Bird in the Bush

Somewhere off the trail in Nootka rose
a skein of song that's unfamiliar
from brush so thick I can't begin
to get through on my own,
some unseen bird
whose name I do not know
is making the true sound
light should make
tumbling through the knothole
of a fence, or a black stone
becoming weightless in the hand.

Finding a Wren's Nest

When our oldest cat left
a dead rat on the ground outside
our window, we watched
for part of a week as a pair
of winter wrens plucked the hairs loose
beak by beak & flew them away.
Efficient wasps removed its eyes,
& red-backed beetles collected
the rest. And here is what's become
of it, wound with moss & bits
of twig, littered with chips of shell,
all stuck behind a loose flap
of cedar bark. To hold a thing like this
in the hand is not to know
ourselves, perhaps, but it's a start.

Rhyme:
Putting an Edge on Things

A farmer grinds his weeding hoe,
    A butcher whets his knives,
A barber strops his razor &
    A hayman stones his scythe.

A woodsman tends his axes,
    A craftsman minds his plane,
A builder keeps his chisels edged,
    A cobbler's blades are keen.

A sawyer files his saw teeth,
    A shepherd hones her shears,
I sharpened up my pencil &
    I wrote this little verse.

Sharpening

Because there is pleasure in cutting,
not tearing the grass, I took our scythe
blade from the snath & laid it
on a length of railroad steel
so that the hammer drew out
the metal, thinned it,
so that when I brought the whetstone down
it sang its raspy way clean across the crescent,
a bright smile,
so that when I swung it
through the high grass
of the orchard it sliced
lightly through the stalks,
which lay in the gentle rows I made,
so that I wondered all morning whether
I was handle, stone, or blade.

Picking Off the Egg Cases

Last summer I paused in my scything
to watch a moth the color of starved butter
whip a froth of eggs on the limb of a plum.
This is what the caterpillar becomes,
& here is its secret waiting.

One of those chores that is casual,
this wandering the orchard in stasis
letting my eye, unfocused slightly, find
the hard foam from twig or branch.
Each unhurried roaming in winter
fills my hand with a dozen.

When I lift the lid of the stove & drop
them in, there's only a quick flash
& a hiss. What I find, I find, what is missed
will hatch hungry in spring,
a nest of writhing things
let loose in the green bliss
of leaves. Against that time
I work in this.

Notes on "Mole Greeting the Sun"

Bronze by Philip McCracken

He has brought everything
into the open, stood it on its hind
legs, tail hanging limp as wet string,
hind claws curved over a base
like the blunt top
of a carrot. Its forepaws are held out
palms open, the way a leaf offers
itself. This is not the moment
of epiphany, but the sole moment
when epiphany is possible, the slope
of its long snout lifted, thrust
forward beyond the tight slits
of its eyes toward something bright
as the wings of a hawk in descent. Shouldn't
we want to be like that, lifting ourselves
out of the dim tunnel of safety,
facing something past
the familiar touch by
which we learned ourselves, declaring
Here am I   Here am I

Old Man Folding a Kerchief in the Supermarket

for Hayden Carruth

He has used it to wipe the filth
from the table where his daughter
has left him to do her shopping
spilling it from the pocket of his jacket
like a small blue lake
the color of an old housedress.

Now he is folding it back into shape
with blunt fingers, hunched
over his labor, watching intently
his hands as though
they might betray him.

For ten minutes this has been
his whole work, & he has gathered
all the deliberate threads
of his attention into this single
act, oblivious to the fact
that anyone might be watching,
that he might be teaching us all
how to live.